365 ways to love your child

365 ways to love your child

TURNING LITTLE MOMENTS INTO LASTING MEMORIES

JULIE LAVENDER

Revell

a division of Baker Publishing Group
Grand Rapids, Michigan

Published by Revell
a division of Baker Publishing Group
PO Box 6287, Grand Rapids, MI 49516-6287
www.revellbooks.com

Printed in the United States of America

Library of Congress Cataloging-in-Publication Data
Names: Lavender, Julie, author.
Title: 365 ways to love your child : turning little moments into lasting memories / Julie Lavender.
Other titles: Three hundred sixty-five ways to love your child.
Description: Grand Rapids, Michigan : Revell, a division of Baker Publishing Group, 2020.
Identifiers: LCCN 2020014981 | ISBN 9780800738846 (paperback) | ISBN 9780800739928 (hardcover)
Subjects: LCSH: Parent and child—Religious aspects—Christianity. | Parenting—Religious aspects—Christianity. | Child rearing—Religious aspects—Christianity.
Classification: LCC BV4529 .L277 2020 | DDC 248.8/45—dc23
LC record available at https://lccn.loc.gov/2020014981

The author is represented by Hartline Literary Agency.

20 21 22 23 24 25 26   7 6 5 4 3 2 1

To the four Js who made me a mommy,
Jeremy, Jenifer, Jeb Daniel, and Jessica—
you will always be my greatest adventure.
My love for you is immeasurable,
and I thank God for you every day.

To David, the love of my life and my best friend—
words can never adequately express my appreciation
for all you've done over the years for our family.
I'll love you forever.

To my heavenly Father—thank you, God,
for unending love, for grace and mercy,
and for the promise of eternity.
Thank you, God, for this book.

contents

1. Elizabeth Barrett Browning, "Sonnet 43: How Do I Love Thee? Let Me Count the Ways," *Sonnets from the Portuguese*, 1850, public domain.

acknowledgments

This book is a tribute to my four children: Jeremy, Jenifer, Jeb Daniel, and Jessica—you are so precious to me, and I love you more than I'll ever be able to express with words or actions. I've enjoyed creating lasting memories with each of you from the moment you were born, and I look forward to so many more! I'll love you forever! I thank you from the bottom of my heart for sharing this life with me! And to my son-in-love, Adam, and my delightful grandson, Benaiah—I am so grateful God added you to our family!

To my husband, David—you are my constant source of encouragement and support. You're my biggest cheerleader, and you never tire of hearing about another one of my writing ideas! Words are inadequate to thank you for all that you've done for my writing journey, our homeschooling journey, and our family. Life with you is a grand adventure, and I'll love you forever and always.

acknowledgments

To all the Blands and Lavenders—thank you for your unending encouragement and support in general and for cheering me on during my writing journey too. I'm so glad to be part of both family trees! I love you guys!

To my agent, Cyle Young, and his wife, Patty—thank you, thank you, thank you! For everything. I don't know where you get all your energy to accomplish all that you do for clients and writers. I'm so glad to be part of your team. You're amazing!

To my editor, Vicki Crumpton—thank you for believing in this book, for patiently encouraging me and offering suggestions in its early stages each time we talked about the manuscript, and for your meticulous care of the words and pages as it became a reality. You are wonderful, and I've so enjoyed this journey with you!

I especially want to thank the Revell team who made this book possible—I am thrilled to be part of the Revell family, and I couldn't have asked for more fabulous folks to work with! I am forever indebted to you!

I want to express my gratitude to writing conference directors in general—I've attended a host of conferences and please know that your hard work doesn't go unnoticed! We writers wouldn't be where we are today without you. I would especially like to recognize two conferences specifically, for without them, the book you hold in your hands probably wouldn't exist. Edie Melson and DiAnn Mills—thank you for Blue Ridge Mountains Christian

Writers Conference. I'll never forget the first time I met with Vicki to talk about my book. Eva Marie Everson and Mark Hancock—thank you for the Florida Christian Writers Conference. I'll never forget Vicki's "yes."

I am indebted to a host of writing friends—iron sharpens iron—and we writers do that so well, don't we? Many of you, I know in person, and many others, only through social media. But to ALL of you, thank you! This journey is better traveled together.

To my special Monketeer writing buddies, Lisa Kibler, Jeannie Waters, and Jean Wilund—thank you for the unending prayers, encouragement, and the constant laughter. And the texts . . . oh, the texts! Good thing I have unlimited texting. And to my longtime girlfriends (and their husbands and kids) Paula Mooney, Elizabeth Webb, Leslie Johnson, Cyd Pagliarullo, and Susan Allen, who helped me raise my kids—thank you! I don't know where they, nor I, would be without your support and prayers and friendship! Love you big!

To the gals of the Serious Writer team, Bethany Jett, Michelle Medlock Adams, and Victoria Duerstock—your writing expertise is unfathomable! Your willingness to share that knowledge with other writers is amazing, and I am forever grateful for your friendship!

To my Guideposts family—wow! I had no idea how my writing journey and community of friends would change after becoming one of the contest winners in 2014! I am so glad to have been added to the family, and I love you all dearly!

I want to express my gratitude to my hometown newspaper family, the *Statesboro Herald* folks, and my editor, Jim Healy—I've enjoyed every freelance contribution and assignment, and I treasure my now-extensive portfolio of local gems!

I am hugely thankful to all the editors I've met and worked with along my writing journey, and I'd like to express my gratitude to Jesse Florea with Focus on the Family's *Clubhouse* magazine; Katy, Beebe, and Rick Kauffman with Lighthouse Bible Studies; Susan King with The Upper Room; Beth Patch with CBN.org; Michelle Cox with Just 18 Summers; Edie Melson with The Write Conversation; Tricia Hodges with The Curriculum Choice; and Amy Milcic with Rock Your Homeschool.

Last, but first in my life, to my heavenly Father—*I've tasted and seen that YOU ARE GOOD* (Ps. 34:8).

introduction

How do I love thee? Let me show thee in many ways
—365 ways, to be exact!

If you're looking for a new way to say "I love you" to your child, turn the page and you'll find 365 suggestions for memory-making moments that will warm your child's heart.

365 Ways to Love Your Child offers creative suggestions for activities, gestures, and expressions of love to show your child how much you treasure them. With simple ideas and heartwarming tokens of affection, *365 Ways* encourages you to spend quality time with your child every day to create a treasury of warm memories to savor throughout childhood and beyond.

With each expression of your love, your child gets a glimpse of the unfathomable love of our heavenly Father. Along the parenting journey, help your child recognize God's love through your own devotion, attentiveness, and verbal affirmations.

Find time each day to transform a little moment into a precious memory. You'll be so glad you did!

ONE

. . . *when we're outside*

- Chase fireflies! On a summer evening, carefully catch one or two or three fireflies in a clean, clear container. Observe closely for a few minutes, then release the lightning bugs in the locations where you found them. Tell your child, "You light up my life!"

- Dress in raincoats and rain boots and play in shallow puddles after showers end.

- Lie on a blanket and watch as the wind moves and changes the puffy, white clouds in the sky. Use your imagination and decide what each cloud resembles. Is it a duck? A tree? A dolphin? When your child has an especially creative sighting, remind them, "I love your imagination!"

- Catch a falling leaf or spiraling seed with your hands or catch a snowflake or raindrop on your tongue.

- Draw a hopscotch pattern on the driveway and play hopscotch. When the pebble lands on a number, tell your child that many things you love about them.

- Give your child a plastic watering can with "I love you" written on it with a permanent marker. Water the plants and flowers and trees together.

- Lie on a blanket on a clear night and look for constellations.

- Play with hula hoops. Learn to keep the hula hoop moving around your waist but get creative too. Have a rolling contest on a sidewalk, driveway, or an open grassy spot to see whose hoop rolls the farthest. Lay the hula hoops in the grass and try to throw Frisbees right in the middle of each hoop. Take turns holding one hula hoop in the air while the other person tosses a ball through the hoop.

- Play with bubbles outside. Use unique, creative bubble wands, such as a clean flyswatter, slotted spoon, small biscuit cutter, small strainer, measuring spoon with open-ended handle, or anything else you care to try.

- Hang out in a hammock on a beautiful afternoon. Read books, sing songs, daydream, reminisce about days gone by, and make up stories with your child in the starring role.

- Take a walk on a sunny afternoon and search for animals. When you locate a critter, share a moment of affection with your little one. For example, a bird sighting means sharing a hug. A squirrel results in a kiss on the cheek. A flitting butterfly warrants butterfly kisses. Seeing another insect means sharing a high five. Decide on other affectionate gestures to share too!

- Play in a sprinkler together on a hot afternoon.

- Go for a walk and pick a bouquet of wildflowers to use as a table centerpiece.

- Wake your child during a late-night meteor shower. Take them outside to lie on a blanket on the ground and watch for falling stars. Tell your child, "You are my shining star!" and "You are out of this world!"

- Go for an outside prayer walk with your child. Pray aloud, thanking God for the provision of a roof over your heads and the love of family. Remind your child that you are so thankful God placed them in your family. Thank God for transportation and safety. Take a stroll through the yard and thank God for his creation. Give thanks for neighbors and pray for them by name.

- Wash the car together on a warm summer day—
and make every effort to get drenched before
the chore is complete!

- Investigate creepy-crawly insects with a
magnifying glass.

- Purchase or check out from the library a book
on bird or tree identification. Go bird-watching
or take a walk in the woods. Use the book to
identify sightings. Talk about the identifying
characteristics of your child—physical, emotional,
and spiritual. Give your child a bear hug and say,
"I love you just the way you are!"

- Plant a tree together in the backyard and watch
it grow over the years. Have picnics on a blanket
near the tree often. Take photos with the tree in
the background, dating each one, and keep the
printed pictures in an album. Look back at the
pictures and reminisce regularly.

- Work together to hang a songbird or
hummingbird feeder outside, preferably in a
spot that is visible from your child's bedroom
window. Say, "Your love gives me wings!" or "You
are tweet!" Remind your child that as much as

you love them, God loves your child even more. Share the meaning of Matthew 10:29, 31: "Are not two sparrows sold for a penny? Yet not one of them will fall to the ground outside your Father's care. . . . So don't be afraid; you are worth more than many sparrows."

- Watch a snail crawl. Look out for the slimy trail it leaves behind! Pretend to be snails and move s-l-o-w-l-y! Say to your child, "Whether you're slow or fast, I shell love you forever!"

- Go for a walk and take a "treasure bag" with you. Carry a backpack, a gallon resealable bag, or an old toiletry bag. Search for unusual pebbles, colorful leaves, wildflowers, odd-shaped sticks, or other unique nature treasures. Collect a few—not more than you can carry home—and treat them as treasures when you return. Have a special place on the counter to display the items and leave them there, if feasible, until the next nature-searching hike.

- Make a string fort. Pick a spot in the yard where four trees are close together and as close to a square shape as possible. Or you can make do with three trees in a triangular shape. Wrap yarn or string around three of the four sides of the square of trees or two sides of the triangle of trees. Wrap enough yarn to make fort walls. Spread a blanket on the ground inside the fort and have a picnic.

- Go on a "silent" nature adventure. Tell your child that you're going to search for nature using only your ears. Take a blanket to the front yard or go for a quiet walk in the woods. Listen for every sound. When you hear something, talk in whispers about what made the sound. Listen for squirrels chittering, leaves rustling, acorns hitting the ground, birds tweeting, crickets chirping, frogs and toads croaking, woodpeckers hammering, creeks gurgling, and hawks calling.

- Ride bikes and trikes and scooters together.

- Hold your child's arms at the wrists and spin around in a circle, lifting their feet off the ground.

- "Fly" your child around the yard. Hold them around the waist with both arms and lift your child in the air, horizontally. Have your child hold their legs together and extend their arms like airplane wings. Run through the yard until someone—parent or child—needs to land!

- Pick dandelions together, the newer ones with yellow flowers and the older ones that have gone to seed. Make a bouquet with the yellow flowers to take home. Hold a seeded-out dandelion for your child to blow the parachute-like seeds. Tell your child you're going to make a silent wish for them and that when you blink three times, it means your wish is complete and says, "I love you." Tell your child to blow on the dandelion. Then let your child hold a dandelion for you to blow and have them think of a wish for you. Tell your child to blink three times for "I love you" when their wish for you is complete.

- Work on outside chores together in every season and turn the work into a fun adventure. Rake fall leaves into a huge pile and jump up and down in the leaves before gathering them in the garbage can. Say, "I can't be-leaf you're mine!" and "I've fallen for you!" Shovel snow together and toss snowballs during the process. Say, "There's snow-body quite like you" and "You melt my heart!" Sweep pollen from the sidewalks in the spring, clean out the flower beds, or plant a garden together. Say, "My love for you grows stronger every year!" Water the lawn together during the summer and pull weeds from the sidewalk. Say, "You warm my heart!" or "You're a cool kid!" or "I'm your biggest fan!"

- Build a dam using large rocks and sticks in a small shallow stream or ditch in the backyard. Be sure to remove the dam when you're finished playing in the pool you created.

- Dig in the dirt. Use fingers and plastic spoons and shovels. Watch for worms!

TWO

. . . *when we're at home*

- Do the dishes together after dinner, then refill the sink with clean, warm water and add dish detergent. Place a sturdy stool in front of the sink for your child to stand next to you and play with water-safe toys in the bubbles!

- Make a tent by spreading a blanket or sheet over the backs of several chairs or the top of a table. Have a picnic or color together inside the tent.

- Go for a prayer walk inside the house, stopping in each room to share aloud related prayers for that room. For example, pray for sweet family time and conversations that are pleasing to God in the dining room. Thank God for his provisions of sustenance in the kitchen. In the den, ask God for reminders to make screen time and music choices that would be pleasing to him. And pray specifically for each family member in that person's bedroom.

- Let your child teach you something they have learned that you're not familiar with, such as a new dance step or sports move or video-game trick.

- Share a favorite memory of your child before prayer time when tucking them into bed and tell

your child why that memory is special. Pleasant
thoughts at bedtime encourage sweet dreams.

• Dry your child's eyes gently when they cry and
never discourage the acknowledgment or display
of feelings. Hold them until the tears subside,
gently stroking your child's hair or rubbing their
back.

• Surprise your sweetie with a warm towel
following bath time. Throw their towel in the
dryer briefly to fluff and warm it for a wintertime
surprise! Remember, never leave a young child
unattended in the bathtub—incorporate the help
of another adult or older child in the house to
accomplish the surprise!

• Quietly arrange some of their toys in a playful
scene, such as setting up a tea party for the
stuffed animals or lining up the cars and trucks
on a pretend highway, while your child slumbers
during the night or takes an afternoon nap.

• Place a fresh flower in a vase of water and sneak
the vase into your child's room while they are
away or taking a nap. Add a love note beside the
flower, such as "You brighten my day" or "You

are special to me" or "I'm glad God picked you for our family."

- Treat your child to a gift for no reason. Hide the surprise somewhere in the house and create scavenger-hunt clues for your child to retrieve the surprise. Write silly notes, such as "Everyone knows how much I love you, and when my nose knows it needs a tissue, you'll find the next clue here." Hide the clue in the bathroom tissue box. Or write, "I chair-ish you. Look under your desk chair for the next clue." When your child finds the gift, say, "I love treating you and giving you gifts and spending time with you. I enjoy showing you how much I love you. But you know what? God loves you so much more than even I love you!"

- Line up chairs in the den in rows of two, like seats on a bus. Climb aboard with your child—let them be the driver—and go on a pretend trip. Talk about what you see out the window or what you will do when you get there. Say to your child, "Even when you drive me nuts, I still love you! In fact, I love you, no matter what!"

- Treat your child to a new pillow or personalized pillowcase. Write a note that says, "Sweet dreams, my sweet!" and place it next to the pillow.

- Be quick to say, "I'm sorry; will you forgive me?" to your child when you make a mistake. Teach them to do the same.

- Acknowledge your child's feelings aloud and be specific. For example, hold your child tenderly and say, "I know you feel sad because you've lost your favorite toy." Or rock your child and say, "I know it hurt your feelings when your friend didn't include you in the game." Or hold your child's hands and jump up and down with them and say, "I know you're excited that you got the part you wanted in the play!"

- Pray often during the day with your child, not just at bedtime. Start the day with prayer, say grace at mealtimes, stop to pray when you hear of a concern, hold your child and pray when they hurt physically or emotionally, and praise God aloud for successes and accomplishments and blessings.

- Pick a day to designate as Backward Day. (This day is officially celebrated in January.) Wear T-shirts backward, pajamas backward, eat breakfast for dinner and dinner for breakfast, carefully walk backward through the house and in the front yard, and practice saying a few sentences backward. What would your name be if spelled backward? M-O-M backward is still M-O-M, and so is D-A-D, but turn first names of family members around and try to pronounce the silly names.

- Link pinkies and make silent wishes when you and your child speak a word or phrase at the same time.

- Make a practice of honking three times when you leave the house to "honk" the words *I love you* to your child if it won't disturb the neighbors.

- Use masking tape on the driveway or another safe paved spot to make a winding, turning path to follow. Take turns walking forward through the path to get to the exit without stepping on the tape. Then walk through the path backward and sideways. Next, try hopping or jumping through the path. Oh, and be sure to let your child help you clean up the tape when you're finished!

- Wear fuzzy socks and slide around on an uncarpeted floor space, pretending to skate. Or skate across the floor with bare feet on top of used dryer sheets. Skate individually and skate holding hands too!

- Keep a personalized water bottle in the refrigerator for your child to grab a swig from throughout the day. Be sure to wash the bottle frequently and refill with ice-cold water. Periodically, tape a new love note to the water bottle.

- Don't discard tattered king-sized pillowcases that need replacing. Take the pillowcases outside and have an old-fashioned sack race.

- Exercise together.

- Snuggle on the couch with your child and flip page by page through your wedding album, sharing memories with your child that include how their parents met and got engaged and special date nights. Or tell stories you've heard about your child's grandparents' newly married days and talk about your life as a child.

- Pull out your child's baby book and retell the story of their birth or adoption. Share milestones and funny stories of infant and toddler days. Give your child a tight hug and say, "I'm so glad you're mine!"

- Turn off the television, computer, or phone and look at your child when they talk to you.

- Headed to the mailbox? No matter how short or long the distance, include your child in the trek. Skip one day, walk backward tomorrow, hop the next day, and jump another day. Retrieve the mail in a zigzag path on occasion and take the long way on another day. Which way is your child's favorite way to get there? Say to your child, "I love you here and there—I love you everywhere!"

- Tell your child about a secret code used during World Wars I and II: an upside-down stamp on a letter meant "I love you." Then turn things upside down for them as your own secret code. When setting the table, turn the silverware upside down at your child's place. Or move your child's pillow to the foot of the bed while they are away. With the lids on tight, flip all the shampoo and soap bottles upside down in your child's shower. You get the idea—get creative!

• Wake your child on a night the moon is full and go for a moonlit walk. Say, "I love you to the moon and back." Add other outlandish measurements of distance, such as "I love you to the bottom of the ocean and back" or "I love you to the top of the tallest tree and back."

• Hide love notes, heart stickers, coins, and small gifts or trinkets in your child's bedroom or bathroom before giving them instructions to clean them. As always, be careful with small items if you have a crawling baby or toddler. Or hide surprises in the glove compartment, drink holders, and other pockets of your car. Hand your child wipes to clean the inside of the car and let them find treats along the way.

• Keep a supply of heart-shaped stickers, hard candies, notes, and trinkets readily available. Don't wait until the need arises, or you'll be caught empty-handed. Share "your heart" with your child frequently: just because, as a reminder, or to cheer up a sad or disappointed youngster.

THREE

. . . when we're in the kitchen

- Eat together as a family: at the kitchen table from take-out boxes, in the den on paper plates and tray tables, or in the dining room on "the good china" for no special reason. Say grace and thank God for your child and the gift of family.

- Involve your child in every aspect of kitchen time. From recipe planning to grocery shopping to cooking to baking to setting the table to doing the dishes—create memories to last a lifetime in the kitchen.

- Treat your child to a lemonade or favorite fruit drink in a disposable cup. Write a love note on the cup and draw hearts with a pen.

- Spell out "I love you" with raisins on a sheet of waxed paper. Then set out small bowls with a spoon in each of nuts, dried fruit pieces, peanut butter chips, pretzels, and cereal pieces. Give your child a resealable bag (with a heart drawn on it) and have them create a bag of trail mix from the trail mix buffet table. After the snacks are prepared, go for a hike along a wooded trail, at a nearby park or playground, or just down the street! Take along water bottles and bags of trail mix.

• Use a scallop-edged biscuit cutter to remove one corner of your child's favorite sandwich. The cut-away piece should look like a bite taken out of the sandwich. (If you don't have a biscuit cutter, use a grapefruit spoon or other small spoon to tear away bite-like marks from one corner.) Write a note that says, "I miss you when we're not together!" and include it in your child's lunchbox along with the sandwich.

• Carefully open the individual sticks of gum in a package and write love notes on the inside of each piece of foil. Tuck the gum back inside the foil wrapping and close completely. Then offer your older child a piece of gum as a surprise!

• Make homemade biscuits and form each one into letters to spell out your child's name.

• Create a written menu, restaurant-style, for the family meal. Some menus may be short and simple, while others may be lengthy and elaborate. Embellish menus with pictures and drawings and love notes written specifically for your child. You might want to come up with creative, silly names for the night's offerings too!

- Finger paint with pudding or yogurt! First, cover the kitchen table with a vinyl tablecloth. Then tear off a large piece of waxed paper for each "artist," including a piece for yourself, and tape the paper securely in place on the tablecloth. Make sure everyone has clean hands, then spoon small dabs of yogurt or pudding onto the waxed paper and let each person use their fingers to create an abstract artwork. Wash or lick fingers clean to create another picture. Work alongside your child to make your own artistic creations. Be sure to write a love note to your child and draw a heart on your "creation" before cleaning up the messy fun.

- Spell "I love you" on a clean table or countertop out of dried beans. Then invite your child to join you in preparing a yummy pot of bean soup for a cold, winter-evening meal. While the soup simmers on the stove, read picture books about soup or a chapter book that takes place in the wintertime.

- Make a honey-do list for your child's chores. Leave the list on the table next to a jar of honey. List chores: clean room, make bed, and so on. Be sure to include these additional chores at the end of the list: "Give me a hug and kiss" and "Meet me in the kitchen for a peanut butter and honey sandwich."

• Wake your child with their favorite breakfast served on two plates—one for them and one for you. Eat breakfast together in bed. You'll probably want to plan this treat for laundry day. After enjoying breakfast, let your child help you strip the bedsheets and carry them to the laundry room.

• Tape a series of love notes on breakfast-making items—on the cereal box, inside the plastic bowl, in the spoon drawer, on the milk jug—if your child is old enough to prepare their own breakfast. Put a few words of a sentence expressing your love and adoration on each note, and when your child has all the necessary breakfast items gathered, they can read the entire sentence.

• Make special pancakes for your love. After mixing the batter, drizzle a small amount from a spoon onto the hot griddle to form the first initial of their name. Be sure to make the letter backward so that it appears right side up when the pancake is flipped. Allow the initial to brown slightly, then pour about one-fourth cup of batter on top of the initial and cook the recommended time for a pancake. Flip the pancake carefully and brown the other side. Serve with syrup or a favorite jam.

- Use cookie cutters to cut baked brownies into shapes that match your child's current interest or a holiday. Save the edges of the brownies in an airtight container to eat as "brownie bites" at another time.

- Remove the edges from two pieces of bread and place the slices on a sheet of waxed paper. Let your child use a rolling pin to flatten each slice. Help your child add deli meat and a slice of cheese on top of each piece of bread. Roll the flattened bread jelly-roll style. Use a dab of softened butter or cream cheese to seal the roll tight. Then enjoy sandwich rolls for lunch! Say to your child, "You are rolls of fun in the kitchen!"

- Purchase a bag of stick pretzels and a bag of knot-shaped pretzels. On a clean table or tablecloth, spell out love messages to each other using the pretzel sticks for straight lines of letters and shapes cut with a plastic knife from the knot pretzels for the curved parts of letters. Then snack on the used pretzels dipped in peanut butter, softened cream cheese, or melted caramel or chocolate.

- Use your favorite layer-cake recipe and add paste food coloring in your child's favorite color to the layers or a different color to each layer. Frost the cake and surprise them during dessert time with the first slice!

- Call ahead to your favorite local pizza parlor and ask the chef to arrange pepperoni slices in the shape of a heart on a pizza. Take your child to the restaurant for lunch and watch their surprise!

- Plan a baking project with your little one. Beforehand, use a thin-lined, black permanent marker to write love notes on the shells of raw eggs, such as "I love you" and "You are egg-ceptional!" and "You are egg-stra special." Then replace the eggs in the carton and return it to the fridge. Ask your child to retrieve the carton of eggs when the recipe calls for them and watch their delight upon opening the container!

- Find out if your local bakery makes letter-shaped donuts. Order donuts for your darling with "I love you" spelled out, along with their name.

- Try a fun seasonal recipe that includes many easy tasks for your child to help with. First, locate a small, decorative jewelry box. Work together to carefully unwrap Hershey's Kisses, placing the chocolates on a platter, tossing the foil wrapper, and storing the Kisses' paper strips in the jewelry box. Say to your child, "I'm saving all my kisses for you!" Preheat oven to 250 degrees. Spread a single layer of Snyder's of Hanover checkerboard-shaped Snaps pretzels on a large baking sheet. Top each pretzel with one chocolate candy. Place the baking sheet in the preheated oven for four minutes. Have your younger child watch as you press holiday-colored M&M's into the warm, almost-melted Hershey's Kisses. Older children who are familiar with hot pans may be able to assist you with this task too. Let the treats cool and then share some with friends or neighbors. And remember to let your child store the "kiss-filled" jewelry box in their room.

- Play a guessing game during an afternoon snack time of animal crackers and milk. Sit at opposite ends of the table with some sort of partition in the middle, such as a stack of books. Each of you will need a selection of the crackers poured onto a sheet of waxed paper. Take turns guessing what animal shape the other person is holding. The guesser can ask only questions that have a yes or no answer. After several rounds, nibble on the cookies. For an extra treat, dip the crackers in various flavors of fruity yogurt.

• Make grilled cheese sandwiches for lunch, using a different type of cheese for each sandwich you make. If it's just you and your child, choose two types of cheese and cut each sandwich in half to share. For more partakers, make additional sandwiches with different cheese slices. Cut each sandwich in half, vertically and horizontally, to form four mini-sandwiches. Let each person try different minis and nibble until they're all gone. Decide which kind of cheese each of you likes best.

• Try a different flavor of milk each week. Let your child help make each recipe with age-appropriate tasks. Make a fruit milk by combining one cup of berries or fruit pieces, one-half cup of sugar, and one-half cup of water in a saucepan. Cook and stir over medium heat until the sauce thickens into a syrup. Strain through a fine-mesh strainer and, when cool, stir into four cups of milk. Chill, then enjoy. Try different fruits each week to change the flavor and color! Or try this warm cinnamon-flavored milk recipe. Heat two cups of milk in a saucepan until very hot. Stir in two teaspoons of honey and four drops of vanilla extract. Let milk cool slightly, then add a pinch of cinnamon just before serving.

• Start the morning with some waffle fun for breakfast. Let your child help you pick out six toppings for waffles, such as fruits sliced into small pieces, miniature chocolate chips, miniature marshmallows, and so on. Place each ingredient in a separate bowl. Number each bowl by attaching a sticky note with a written numeral one through six. Place cooked and cooled waffles on plates, one for each of you. The object of the game is to be the first person to have four of the same topping pieces in a row, horizontal, vertical, or diagonal, in the tiny square indentions of the waffle. Take turns rolling a die. The number on the die tells the player which topping to add to their waffle. Who says you can't play with your food?

- Create a dessert that'll put a smile on your child's face! Let your child help you make a batch of instant chocolate pudding, following the directions on the package. While the pudding chills, sneak back into the kitchen, unroll a sheet of refrigerated pie crust, and lay it flat on a slightly greased baking sheet. Use a knife to cut and remove circles in the dough for eyes and to make a U-shaped smile cutout. Brush melted butter on the smiling pie crust and bake in a 375-degree oven for ten minutes or until golden brown. When the crust cools, ask your child to join you in the kitchen to see the smiley-face crust. Break off pieces to dip into a small amount of pudding for a snack. If desired, make a recipe of homemade applesauce instead of pudding and enjoy pie crust dipped into warm applesauce.

- Sip warm milk or hot cocoa next to the fireplace or bundled up in coats and mittens on the front-porch steps during the winter. Eat popsicles under a shady tree during the summer. Slurp apple cider on a blanket in the fall. Drink lemonade or fruit punch at a picnic table in the spring.

• Celebrate an accomplishment with a confetti breakfast for dinner. First, prepare a confetti fruit bowl by combining slices of fruit in a variety of colors. Use fresh and frozen fruit to get the desired effect. Give your child the age-appropriate task of slicing or stirring. Then make confetti pancakes together. Follow the directions on a pancake mix to make the batter and add a tablespoon of rainbow-colored jimmies, sometimes called sprinkles, before cooking. When the pancakes are slightly cooled, spread a thin layer of vanilla frosting on top of each pancake and sprinkle a few more jimmies on top. Celebrate with confetti fruit and confetti pancakes!

• Use drops of food coloring to give new shades to food items according to the season. For example, try pink milk in February, green scrambled eggs in March, pastel-colored mashed potatoes in April, school-bus-yellow grits in August, fall-colors sprinkled cookies in September, orange rice in October, and red-and-green chicken salad sandwiches in December.

- Make a chocolate-chip-cookie pizza with candy pieces as toppings for a special occasion or celebration. Use refrigerated chocolate-chip-cookie dough or a homemade recipe to bake a rectangular-shaped cookie on a sheet cake pan according to directions found online. (You can also use a pizza pan, but you'll need one with sides to keep the crust from rising and spilling over.) While the cookie cake is baking, the adult should chop favorite candy bars into small pieces. Let your child place the pieces in separate bowls to prepare a buffet of favorite candy toppings. When the oven timer buzzes, remove the cookie cake and place on hot pads. With directions from your child, top their section of the cookie cake with selected candy pieces from the buffet bowls. Add the toppings you want to your section. Place the cookie cake back in the oven for about three or four minutes for the candy pieces to soften and melt.

FOUR

. . . when we're running errands

- Play a grocery store game: ask your child to try to spot grocery items that begin with each letter of the alphabet. At home, let your child help you unload the groceries you purchased, and be sure to say, "I love how you help me with chores!"

- Walk with arms linked with an older child or carry a younger child piggyback when completing simple errands.

- Allow time between errands to fit in a playground visit. Stop at a nearby park and swing or slide with your child—don't just be a bystander or a benchwarmer—before resuming errands.

- Gather toy trucks and work vehicles to play with and walk or drive to a nearby construction site. Sit on the ground or in the car at a safe distance and location from the construction site and enjoy watching the men and women at work. Talk about what chores they are accomplishing and what tools they are using. Use your imagination to guess what they are building if you don't already know. You might even want to make up a silly story about the construction

site, such as, "What would happen if three friends—a turtle, a mouse, and a skunk—moved into the unfinished building overnight?"

- Occasionally, walk your child all the way to the bus stop or classroom or baseball field instead of just watching from the front door or dropping off and waving from the car. Give a lingering hug and huge kiss and say, "I can't wait to hear all about your day when I see you again!"

- Preorder a decorated cookie cake from a local bakery. Have the decorator inscribe the words, "I love you" and include your child's name. Let the clerks know when you'll pick up the cake and ask them to display it in the glass case at eye level. Tell your child you're stopping by the bakery after running errands and let your child find the surprise when you arrive.

- Pick out one of your child's favorite snacks and write "I love you" or draw a heart on the package or attach a sticky note to a snack container and juice box. Bring the snack in the car when you pick up your child from daycare or school or the sitter. This simple act lets your child know you've been thinking about them.

- Share jokes, riddles, knock-knock jokes, and tongue twisters while riding in the car to run errands. In other words, laugh a lot with your child! Remember to say often, "You make me so happy!"

- Search for objects in alphabetical order during lengthy errands. Look for an animal, a baseball field, a coffee shop, and so on. At the end of running errands, give your child a big hug or squeeze and say, "Thank you for helping me run errands! I love you from A to Z, and I'm so glad you were with me today!"

- Be an active part of your child's education. If you're a homeschooling family, say to your child often, "I love teaching you!" If your child attends daycare or school, visit regularly to eat lunch. Make appointments with their teacher to chat positively about your child. Let your child help you pick out gifts and trinkets to give to their teacher. Be sure to let your child add sweet notes of appreciation with each gift and sign your name to the card also. If possible, never miss a performance or play or book fair. Volunteer in the classroom or school library or lunchroom. When the class photo comes home, make a concerted effort to learn every child's name in the class. Let your child know you value everything about their education. And when your child comes home with completed papers or projects, say, "You are a great student!" or "I think you're so smart!" or "I really like that you put your best effort into schoolwork!"

• Count the train cars when you're stopped at a railroad crossing. When the last car passes by, look your child in the eye and say, "I will always choo-choose you to be mine!"

• Have your child bathe and put on their pajamas. Then don yours too and load up in the family car for a nighttime snack run. Drive to a fast-food spot with a drive-up window and order a bedtime snack. You'll want to pick a place with good nighttime snack options. If the restaurant is one of those carhop-style places, park in one of the stalls to order. Snack in the car and read bedtime stories aloud before leaving. Drive back home slightly past bedtime, but don't forget to brush your teeth when you return!

• Toss pennies in a fountain and make wishes, but with this caveat: you make wishes for your child and your child makes wishes for you. Take turns sharing the wishes aloud and tossing pennies.

- Visit the library often and read several books before leaving the premises. Get to know the children's librarians personally and greet them by name with each visit. Tell the librarian about your child's current interests and have them help you find books to match those interests.

- Pick out cues as prayer reminders for others when you run errands. For example, pray for pastors and ministers when you pass a church. Pray for ambulance drivers and patients when you spot an ambulance. Pray for children when you drive by a park. Pray for teachers when you see a school.

- Write a letter to a cousin or grandparent or friend, seal it in an envelope, and drive to the post office to mail the letter. On the drive to the post office, share things you love most about that person and favorite memories of time spent with them. Remind your child, "I'm so glad you're part of my family!"

- Take your child to the bank with you and open a savings account in their name. Talk about the value of saving money. Each time your child receives a monetary gift, help them deposit some of the cash into the savings account, some into a piggy bank for short-term savings, and some into a donation envelope for tithing. Say to your child on the way to the bank, "You can always count on my love!" and "I'll love you forever—you can take that to the bank!"

- Compliment your child on their appearance while out and about. Say, "You look very pretty/ handsome today. But you know what else? You are even more beautiful on the inside, and that's the best part!"

- Ride the escalator up and down just to spend extra time with your child. Take the elevator all the way to the top floor, no matter the destination. Take an extra spin in the revolving door, just because. Give your child's hand a squeeze and say, "I love spending time with you!"

- Embellish a pair of sunglasses for each of you to wear on the next errand run. Choose sunglasses with ample rim and arm space for decorating. Cover the workspace adequately and wear old clothes. Paint designs with colored nail polish or glue on beads, pearls, plastic flowers, or decorative buttons. An adult will need to use superglue to stick the items on, but a child can point out the desired location of the embellishment.

- Keep a kitchen baking sheet in the car and give your child fun magnets to create stories as you run errands. (Make sure the magnets stick to the baking sheet before storing it in the car!)

- Play an imaginary game of hide-and-seek while running errands. Let your child think of a hiding spot inside a house. Because it's a pretend game, the location can be anywhere and any size. Ask them questions that can be answered yes or no and try to guess the hiding spot. You take a turn next and let your child guess your hiding spot.

- Use hot glue or superglue to secure a baseplate for plastic building blocks to the inside of a medium-sized storage container lid. Make sure to buy age-appropriately—baseplates with larger pegs for young builders eighteen months to four or five years old and baseplates with smaller pegs for builders six and older. The smaller building blocks are choking hazards for young children. Once the glue has dried and the baseplate is held tight, fill the box with a variety of building blocks. While out and about running errands, your child can securely construct a design on the baseplate.

- Play a silly game of "Would you rather?" with your child. Ask questions, such as "Would you rather sleep in a hammock in the top of a tree or sleep in a bathtub filled with marshmallows?"

- Arrange ahead of time to tour a fire station. On the return drive, discuss fire safety at home and tell your child that their safety is important to you because you love them. Come up with a fire-escape plan for your home, establish a meeting place outside, and rehearse a fire drill.

- Let your child see you pray for others. While out and about, if someone shares a prayer request or concern, stop right then and pray on the spot, including your child in the prayer huddle. Before saying grace in a restaurant, tell your server you're about to say grace and ask if they have a request or concern.

- Take part in a scavenger hunt while running errands. Keep paint strips from a paint or department store in the car. Let your child match colors of sights seen while driving. Or keep a package of magnetic letters and a baking sheet handy. Help your child alphabetize the letters on the tray. When they spot a letter on a sign or billboard, ask your child to remove that letter from the baking sheet. What letters are left at the end of the errands?

- Play "What if?" while riding in the car to incorporate sights seen through the windows. Ask your child questions and let them create serious or outlandish stories or scenarios to answer the question. For example, ask, "What if you were as tall as that building?" or "What if you had leaves for hair?" or "What if every animal we see today followed us home?"

- Take along a favorite toy or stuffed animal on a day filled with many errands. Allow time at each stop to snap a selfie with you, your child, and the favored toy. Try to pick backgrounds that give details of your location. Make a few pit stops along the way, just for fun, to take additional selfies, such as at a downtown fountain or a neighborhood park or a local vendor's flower bed. Together, make up pretend stories about the stuffed animal's or favorite toy's adventures when you get home. Invite your child to write the story, illustrate their ideas, or record a verbal narrative of the day.

• Make a stop at a weekend farmers market or visit a you-pick field or orchard. Enjoy selecting vegetables and berries and fruits together. Use the fresh-picked produce in a recipe when you get home.

FIVE

... when we're playing games

- Be your child's biggest cheerleader at every sporting event. Point out the good plays and great sportsmanlike-conduct moments and don't focus on the missed goals or mistakes. If you're the coach, find a gentle way to correct or reprimand if necessary.

- Reward extracurricular effort and attempts with compliments, hugs, high fives, edible treats, and small tangible tokens. Brag on your child's perseverance and teamwork and point out teammates' accomplishments too, teaching your child to support and encourage others.

- Make whatever sport your little athlete is into for the season a priority during family playtime. Organize a game of soccer, T-ball, or basketball with neighborhood kids or cousins. And plan to visit a local recreational-league game or a high school, college, or professional team competition of that sport as well.

- Inflate and tie securely a balloon for both of you if your child is at the appropriate age. Have your child use a permanent marker to write a love note on your balloon, and you do the same with their balloon. (Be careful with permanent markers— wear old clothes and cover the work area with an old tablecloth.) When you're sure the marker has dried completely, play with the balloons in the den. See who can keep the balloon afloat the longest without it touching the floor. Try unique ways to keep the balloon in the air, such as using only one elbow or both knees or the inside of one wrist or another creative method.

- Invite your child to wrap their arms around your waist and stand on top of your shoes. Hug your child and walk around the house. See how long you can walk without the little one's feet slipping off. On another day, try a similar walking game outside. Have your child stand on your shoes with their back against your legs. Hold on to your child's hands, arms, or shoulders and go for a walk in the grass.

- Save and wash ten empty plastic liter bottles. Use a permanent marker to write short love notes on each bottle—for example, "I love you," "You are special to me," "You are sweet," "You are kind," "You make me happy," and so on. Line up the empty bottles in a bowling pin arrangement on a flat surface, such as in an uncarpeted room or outside on the driveway. Stand one bottle in front, two bottles in the second row, three in the third, and four in the last row. Take turns with your child rolling a large bouncing ball toward the empty bottles. Let your child read the love messages on the bottles they knock over, tally the number of downed bottles for the score, and then reset the bottles for another round of play.

- Have a snowball fight in the comfort of your home with recycled sheets of paper. Let your child help wad up dozens of sheets of used paper into "snowball" sizes. Use a long piece of yarn to divide the room into two sections and sort the snowballs evenly between the two of you. Play Christmas music or use a favorite playlist of songs. When the song begins, each person tosses "snowballs" at the other person. Tossing continues while the music plays. When the song ends, the person with the least snowballs on their side of the yarn is the "snowball" champion!

- Teach your child how to play your favorite sport or game and then include them on some of those excursions, just the two of you. If you golf with friends occasionally, have a golf date with just your child. If you play an online computer game for relaxation, usually after your child goes to bed, show your child how to play the game and let them sit next to you while you play. If you and your spouse play cards on date night, teach your child how to play the same game and let them have a chance at a round or two.

• Create an obstacle course in the backyard with your child's help. Stand a folding chair in the grass to crawl through; place a short, sturdy stool to scale and leap from; curl a garden hose to jump over; and line up a dozen cups or cones to weave between. You can even set up the obstacle course near a swing set with a slide and include it as part of the course.

• Use an online program to create a personalized crossword puzzle with clues and answers about your child: favorite color, name of stuffed animal, age, recent vacation, and so on. Print out the puzzle and then work together to complete it.

• Create a personalized game of Memory by printing out double copies of twelve pictures of your child. Include pictures of both of you, pictures with friends or other family members, vacation pictures, and so on. Glue the twenty-four pictures onto playing cards from an incomplete set. Once the glue is completely dry, turn the two dozen cards facedown on the floor, mix them up well, and play the game by turning over two cards in a turn. A match results in an extra turn, and the person with the most matched pairs at the end of the game is the winner. When your child gets a match, say, "You're really good at this game!" or "Wow, you're really concentrating!" or "You're doing a great job of paying attention to the cards!"

- Save water bottle caps until you've collected a dozen or more. Write your initial with a permanent marker on half of the caps and your child's initial on the other half. Use low-tack painter's tape to make a rectangular-shaped, mock shuffleboard pattern on the floor or kitchen table. Take turns "flicking" a bottle cap, sending it sliding across the table or floor. The object is to get as many bottle caps in the highest scoring area as possible.

- Make homemade bean bags from mismatched socks for a fun game of tic-tac-toe. Fill the toes of eight to ten old socks, preferably in two different colors. Wrap rubber bands tightly around each bean-filled toe area, leaving the rest of the sock for a "handle." Use rope or yarn to make a large tic-tac-toe board in the grass. Take turns tossing the socks toward the board to see who can score three in a row first. When your child wins, yell, "Tic-tac-toe—I love you so!" and give them a high five.

• Play baseball with an inflated beach ball and a plastic bat. When either of you crosses home plate for a run, make sure there are plenty of high fives and "I love yous."

• Save and wash plastic lids from store-bought food items, such as frozen whipped topping, sour cream, pimento cheese, or soft butter spreads. Write love notes on each lid with a permanent marker. Then take your child outside to play with the lids like Frisbees on a breezy afternoon and let your child read the messages when they toss or retrieve them. For added fun, place a laundry basket on the ground outside and see if you can toss the lids into the basket.

- Grab brooms—one adult-sized and one kid-sized—and two tennis balls and head to the driveway. You can also play this game on a paved area in a nearby park or an unoccupied basketball court. Use masking tape to designate a goal or, for a more challenging option, turn a laundry basket on its side and prop it in place with large books. Use the brooms to sweep and push the tennis balls from one end of the playing area to the goal line. Say to your child, "I love playing games with you!"

- Tightrope walk in the backyard. Stretch out a long jump rope in the grass. Extend your arms horizontally and walk heel-touching-toe over and over to reach the other end. Can you make it without stepping off the rope? What about backward or sideways?

- Fill a resealable gallon bag with low-sugar, whole-grain cereal pieces; fresh bread crusts cut into bite-size pieces; pumpkin seeds; and other safe food bits that birds or squirrels would enjoy. Go for a walk in the woods or along a walking trail that has several path options. Make a game out of the hike by dropping food bits along the way. At some

point, turn around and follow the trail of
crumbs back to the car.

• Have a stick-boat race in a small, nearby stream
  or in a fast-moving trail of water against the curb
  of your street after a very rainy day. (Be sure to
  keep safety in mind around water or traffic.) If you
  don't have a stream nearby, dress appropriately
  and jump in a puddle in the backyard!

• Follow the family dog or cat around the house or
  backyard and make up a story as you go. Pretend
  the family pet is solving a mystery or searching
  for treasure or exploring a new planet. Make
  up scenes and sentences to go along with the
  adventure! Remind your child as you wander, "I
  love how well you take care of our family pet!"

• Take part together in a community charitable
  run or walk. Whether you're a runner or a walker,
  sign up for the event and explain to your child
  in detail the purpose of the benefit. If possible,
  choose a fundraiser that has a personal meaning
  to your child, such as a breast cancer walk if your
  child's grandmother is a breast cancer survivor
  or a homeless-shelter benefit if your child has a
  classmate who is a shelter resident.

- Learn to jump rope. Purchase two individual-length jump ropes so that the two of you can practice jumping at the same time. Also purchase a longer rope from a school catalog or an online source. To master the longer rope, start by jumping over an immobile rope on the ground. Next, let two people swing the rope slowly back and forth close to the ground and have the third person jump over it while it is moving. Older children can learn to jump rope while two people turn the rope in a complete circle.

- During the week, toss all dirty socks, unmatched, into a laundry basket. After the laundry is done, let your child help match and tuck socks together, then toss matched socks into an empty basket on the floor. Once the matching and tossing game is complete, have each person gather their socks and carry them to their bedroom.

- Play balloon volleyball. Tie a piece of yarn or string between two chairs. Bat a balloon back and forth with your hands, keeping it off the floor. For an extra challenge, keep two balloons going at the same time.

• Crisscross several strips of low-tack painter's tape across the top of an open doorway. Tape on both sides of the doorway so that the sticky side faces both directions. Wad up torn pieces of newspaper. Let your child toss newspaper wads from one side of the door frame, while you toss from the other side. You'll need to throw while seated and your child can stand or sit. The person with the most wads stuck to the sticky side of the tape facing them is the winner.

• Use swimming pool noodles and a perforated plastic ball outside like a game of hockey. Use masking tape to mark off a goal on the driveway and then take turns sending the ball toward the goal by bopping it with a pool noodle.

• Play a game with a twin sheet and a conglomeration of balls. Hold two corners of the sheet and have your child hold the opposite two corners. Fill the sheet with a combination of ping-pong balls, bouncy balls, and other lightweight balls. Shake the sheet up and down but try to catch and keep all the balls inside the sheet.

• Use a world globe or map for this fun game. But first, prepare a prop you'll use later.

Fold construction paper or computer paper, accordion style, the width of a gingerbread-child cookie cutter. Trace around the cookie cutter and cut out the pattern, making sure the hands of the pattern are on the fold and left uncut. Unfold the cutout shapes and you'll have a string of gingerbread kids holding hands. Put the paper aside for now. Let your child spin the globe slowly and trace their finger on the globe as it spins. When the globe stops moving, locate the country or state that your child's finger is touching. If you're using a map, have your child trace their finger on it, with eyes closed, until you say "Stop." Use reputable online websites to learn about that country, especially bits of trivia about the kids in that country—what they do for fun, whether they wear uniforms to school, what kinds of festivals and holidays they celebrate, and so on. Work together with your child to "dress" one of the gingerbread shapes to resemble a child from that country. Use markers, scraps of cloth, or stickers. Write the name of the country on the back of the shape. Play the game again on a different day and embellish another shape to resemble a youngster from the new country on which your child's finger landed. Continue exploring other countries until the hand-holding string of kids is complete.

Remind your child that God loves people and that
God wants us to love others too. Share
this verse: "Beloved, let us love one
another, for love is from God,
and whoever loves has been
born of God and knows God"
(1 John 4:7 ESV).

SIX

. . . when we're getting creative

- Color side-by-side pictures together in a coloring book. At some point during the creative moment, say, "Wow—you're a great artist!"

- Make up a tongue twister with your child's name. Use as many words as possible in the sentence with the same first letter as the first letter of your child's name, but make sure the sentence makes sense. Then both of you try to say it three times fast!

- Display your child's artwork in a prominent place in the home. Use a magnet to place the masterpiece on the fridge, lean the artwork against a picture frame and place it in the center of the table as a centerpiece, or hang twine on a wall or across a window in the child's room like a clothesline from one side to the other and attach artwork pieces to the line with clothespins. Switch out older pieces with new ones frequently. Save as many pieces of creativity as you have the room to house, but if space is at

a premium, snap a picture of each piece of art before discarding it.

• Dress up in silly clothes and have a dance party. Dance to a variety of musical styles and sing along with the songs you recognize.

• Make up a silly song about your child. Sing it to the tune of a familiar children's song if you lack ideas for a melody. Teach the song to your child while sitting in a rocking chair or swaying on a porch swing. Sing the silly song while dancing or twirling with your child and repeat the silly creation while tucking your child in bed at night. Make sure to include a chorus with words that express how much you love your child.

• Create a family tree on a sheet of poster board that includes great-grandparents, grandparents, parents, siblings, aunts, uncles, and cousins. Write out the names of each family member and include small pictures next to the names. Let your child write their name with a favorite color of marker in the correct place and then use a red marker to enclose your child's name inside a heart shape. Remind your child how thankful you are that they are part of your family. Place the family tree poster in the child's room and use it as a visual reminder to pray for family members by name at bedtime.

- Pick a favorite song and make up dance steps to go along with the music. Design hand motions too. Then each time you hear the song on the radio at home, stop what you're doing and dance. Or if the song plays while in the car, break out in the hand motions and sing loudly. If you happen to be the driver, however, keep both hands on the wheel!

- Create a dot-to-dot page for your sweetie. Arrange numbered dots in the shape of a large heart. On the inside of the heart and using capital letters, arrange numbered dots in the shape of the first letter of your child's name and your name. Draw a plus sign between the two letters. Leave the dot-to-dot secret message on your child's pillow or at their place at the dinner table as a surprise.

- Make a bookmark from craft paper. Glue a picture of you and your child at the top and below it write, "I love you from beginning to end." Laminate the bookmark or cover it with clear contact paper. Punch a hole near the top and knot a piece of favorite-color yarn through the hole. Hide the bookmark in your child's Bible, schoolbook, or favorite chapter book.

- Build a log cabin together by gluing wooden craft sticks onto four sides of a small, square box. Once the glue is dry, use a marker to draw a door and windows. Fold a piece of construction paper for the roof and attach with tape. Say to your child, "Home is wherever you are!" or "I'm glad you're in my family!"

- Create a family newspaper with your child once a month or bimonthly to update faraway relatives and friends. Let your child contribute recent events and accomplishments in their life and be sure to share other family happenings too. Send the newspaper via email or print out copies and let your child help you address envelopes and drop them in the mailbox. When friends and family respond with their own updates and happenings, be sure to read them together with your child.

- Give your child lessons in your favorite hobby and work together on occasion. Do you crochet?

Teach your child some simple crochet patterns. Do you collect stamps? Share your collection and talk about how long you've been collecting. Do you restore vintage automobiles? Include your child in simple repair jobs and be sure to explain the names and purposes of the tools you're using.

- Make puppets and get creative. Ideas abound online but consider making puppets out of paper bags, socks, pom-poms and pipe cleaners, construction paper, paper plates, Styrofoam cups, and so much more. Make new puppets each month and then brainstorm a play using the creations. Keep the designs together after each play finale  and, next month, make up another act to include the new cast of characters. Throughout the month, discuss upcoming plotlines while waiting in line at the grocery checkout, bus stop, or traffic light.

- Make homemade modeling dough and let your child help measure ingredients. Recipes can be found online, and some even suggest adding scents or glitter. Test the temperature of the dough and join your child in creating with the dough while it's still warm.

- Teach your child the joy of giving creative homemade gifts. Start with three long, thin scarves. Bunch the three together and tie a knot near one end. Working on a table or on the floor, teach your child how to braid. Hold the knotted end and help your child tighten the scarves with each crossover. Let your child braid the scarves to the end and tie a knot at that end of the braid. Wear your new scarf proudly, and say to your child, "I think of you every time I look at my scarf!" Or prepare the scarf as a gift for someone else and say, "I know she'll think of you every time she wears this scarf!" For a smaller project, help your child braid three strips of yarn to make a bookmark.

- Write a poem for your child, expressing your love or extolling their virtues. Your poem may be serious or silly. Read the poem to your child and then, depending on their age, write a poem together or encourage them to write you a poem. Try your hand at rhyming verse, free verse, haiku, and limericks. Remind your child that as much as you love them, God loves your child even more! Commit to memory 1 Chronicles 16:34: "Give thanks to the LORD, for he is good; his love endures forever."

- Grab two flashlights, dim or turn off the den lights, turn on the radio, and lie on the floor in sleeping bags at bedtime. Shine the flashlights on the ceiling and let the light beams dance to the music. After the performance, turn off the lights and slumber together on the den floor.

- Purchase a kit or build, paint, and hang a birdhouse together for winged visitors. Talk about being grateful to have a roof over your head, pray for those who do not, and think of some ways that you can assist the homeless or a homeless shelter in your area.

- Try out this fun craft and then share the final product as a gift. Steep several tea bags in a large pot, following package directions. Set the pot aside for at least fifteen minutes. Let your child help you wet and wring out white cotton handkerchiefs. After an adult carefully removes and discards the tea bags, help your child use a long-handled spoon to submerge the handkerchiefs in the pot of tea. Soak the submerged handkerchiefs for at least one hour. Drain the pot and rinse the handkerchiefs in cold water. Soak the handkerchiefs in a pot of cold water for ten minutes. Wring out the excess water and let dry in a sunny area outside. Once the handkerchiefs are completely dry, place several unused tea bags in the center of a handkerchief, gather up the extra material, and tie closed with a pretty ribbon. Give the gift to a favorite tea drinker and be sure to whisper in your child's ear, "You're my cup of tea" or "You are tea-rific!"

- Create an abstract masterpiece with broken and used crayons. Purchase a canvas board from a craft store. Use a potato peeler or metal cheese grater to strip off shavings of various colors. Scatter some of the shavings onto the canvas and set the canvas outside in the hot sun. Tilt the canvas slightly so the melted shavings will drip down the canvas. For easy cleanup, be sure to place the canvas on a piece of cardboard. After a couple of hours, scatter additional shavings and lean the canvas in a different direction. Add shavings throughout the hot afternoon and then bring the artwork inside to cool and harden.

- Create a new handprint craft each month and watch how the size of your child's handprint changes over the years. A heaping handful of handprint art projects can be found online, from peacocks to trees, smiling suns, elephants, angels, and much more. Be sure to say to your child often, "I've gotta hand it to you—you are one cool kid!"

- Take part in a community play together. If acting is not your thing, volunteer to hand out programs or collect tickets together instead.

- Visit an art show or exhibit. Then create some masterpieces of your own, either working together or individually. Title the works and invite friends and family over to see the exhibit.

- Create fingerprint art projects from easy instructions and samples online. Talk about the uniqueness of fingerprints and say to your child, "You are unique and that's why I love you so!" or "You are one of a kind!" Help your child memorize Psalm 139:14: "I praise you because I am fearfully and wonderfully made; your works are wonderful, I know that full well."

• Visit a pottery store and work on a project together. Create something you'll use at home, such as a holiday platter, and be sure to sign your names and the date of completion on the back.

• Visit a planetarium. Then use silver or gold star stickers on black construction paper to create familiar constellations or make up some new ones! Tell your child, "You are so bright!"

• Make a flower chain from a patch of flowering weeds. Pick about ten flowers, leaving a four-inch stem. With a fingernail or toothpick, make a slit about three inches below the bud and thread the stem of another flower through. Make a similar slit in the second flower and attach another one. Continue until you've used all the flowers. Carefully loop the last stem around the first flower and tie a knot with the stem.

• Make a mud pie. Use rocks or leaves or berries to embellish the mud pie with the first initial of your child's name.

• Paint! Paint with brushes, cotton swabs, toothbrushes, sponges, plastic silverware, or fingers. Outdoors, dip a flyswatter in a shallow paint container and splatter the paint on a large sheet of paper. Roll washable, toy vehicles in paint and make tracks on art paper. Dip plastic animals in paint and make footprints on paper. When your child finishes a masterpiece, say, "I think you're so creative!" or "You are a talented kid!"

• Paint and decorate large, smooth rocks. But first, wash the rocks in mild detergent, rinse well, and dry completely. Use acrylics (or paint recommended for porous surfaces). Add the painted rocks to flower beds for décor.

• Create music with wooden spoons and other household items, such as inverted pots and pans, plastic bowls turned upside down, lids, or empty cereal and oatmeal boxes. Add other musical sounds by shaking coins tightly secured in a plastic container, beads or buttons in a small storage container, or uncooked rice in a taped-closed, plastic Easter egg.

SEVEN

. . . when we're reading and playing

- Read, read, read. Repeat. Read books every day with your child—in the morning, at naptime, while waiting for an appointment, at bedtime, and in between. Let them catch you reading. Sit on the couch next to your independently reading child and read simultaneously, but don't give up reading aloud to your already-reading child either.

- Look at family photo albums together and reminisce. Say to your child, "We have so many fun family memories, don't we?" or "We really know how to have fun, don't we?"

- Play with small bouncy balls in the largest room of the house.

- Combine two or three board-game playing pieces and boards and make up rules for a new game. As you clean up together, tell your child this silly pun: "I'm never board when I'm with you!"

- Purchase a package of inexpensive, plastic parachute toys to use on a windy day. Make sure to have extras in case the wind carries some away or the strings get tangled. When the wind picks up, take the toys to a nearby playground or play in the backyard. Toss the parachute toys while standing safely atop one of the playground equipment pieces or launch them from an open spot in the yard.

- Use large towels and large safety pins to make capes for you and your child. Then share what superhuman powers each of you possess. Tell your child why you think they are a superhero.

- Read a book together in a dark room, under the bedsheets, with a flashlight. Read outside in a fort or in the shade of a tree. Read inside in a tent made of sheets and blankets. Read anywhere!

- Purchase a puzzle to assemble together that has an appropriate number of pieces for your child's age. Pour the pieces onto a table and arrange them in a heart shape. Leave a note next to the heart that says, "We fit together nicely!" Then find an afternoon to work together to complete the puzzle or work on it a few minutes every night before bedtime until the puzzle is complete.

- Have a toy-washing day. Clean washable toys outside by filling a wading pool or large container with water and dish detergent. Scrub and wash toys clean, then spread them out on the driveway and let your child use a garden hose to rinse away the suds.

- Start an imaginary story with your child as the main character. Take turns adding to the story with creative ideas and adventures.

- Use your imagination to take stuffed animals on a fun adventure in the den. Both of you will need a teddy bear or stuffed animal. Let your child take the lead to help the stuffed animals crawl across the couch, leap to a chair, and scale the side of the entertainment center. Help your "adventurers" get from one side of the room to the other without touching the floor.

- Play with your child every day, even if a busy schedule leaves only a few minutes for playtime on some days. Play a board game, use your imagination outside, or play inside with toys—but allow playtime opportunities daily. And as often as possible, make sure to devote a large portion of the day to uninterrupted playtime.

- Save and collect boxes of all sizes: cardboard boxes received in the mail, empty cereal and pasta boxes, gift boxes, and so on. Once you've amassed enough boxes, build towers and skyscrapers in the den. Who can build the tallest building? Make stacks and then roll a large plastic ball into the boxes and watch them scatter.

- Make paper airplanes, following online instructions or by creating your own patterns. Stand on the front porch or the top step of a stepstool in the grass and launch the airplanes.

- Play this fun game every day for a week or every other day for a couple of weeks. Purchase a large package of inexpensive floating rubber ducks. Use a permanent marker to write numerals on the bottom of each duck. Then make a matching list of treats for each number. For example, duck number two might be a lollipop prize. Duck number four might be instructions for your child to do four jumping jacks for four kisses. Duck number six might be an extra story at bedtime. Fill an outside wading pool with water and the numbered ducks. To help the ducks "swim," you or your child can run around the outside of the pool while dragging a large spatula or wooden spoon through the water. The ducks will travel in a circle with the swirling water. Then let your child "catch" swimming ducks to get a prize. Drape a tarp or old sheet over the top of the pool to keep the water clear as you play the game over the next week or two.

- Place a large tablecloth or sheet on the den floor. Fill a medium-sized storage container to approximately three-fourths full with raw rice. Add measuring spoons and cups, plastic trucks and cars, shovels and small bowls, and other scooping tools to the container. Sit on the floor and play with your child, measuring and exploring creative options with the rice. When finished playing, carefully return any rice that fell on the tablecloth or sheet back into the storage container and cover securely with a plastic lid for another day of playtime.

- Keep abreast of your child's current interests. Supply books and toys from the library, bookstore, or dollar store to encourage your child's education and creativity. Dinosaurs this week? A wealth of fiction and nonfiction books about these extinct creatures exist. Sea creatures next month? Look for books about sharks, sea anemones, coral, sea turtles, dolphins, whales, plankton, and more. Astronauts? Find books that are "out of this world" for your child. Foster their inquisitive nature with books and inexpensive toys. Say to your child, "I love watching you learn new things!"

• Choose one of your child's favorite picture books and order an extra copy of the story, in paperback, if possible. Print out copies of your child's face from a favorite photo and paste it over the face of the main character of the story. Use a permanent marker to change the name of the character in the book to your child's name and have fun reading the story over and over with your child as the main character!

• Encourage your child to read age-appropriate chapter books on their own but get a second copy for you to read so that you can talk together about the characters and plot. Can you guess what will happen in the next chapter? Can you solve the mystery before the end?

- Order pencils in your child's favorite color or other trinkets with their name printed on them. Consider stamping "I love you" on them too.

- Learn to juggle as a family with simple household items. Online tutorials teach juggling skills for beginners and beyond! Juggle with scarves or adult socks. Tie a knot in the center of each scarf and each sock. Younger children will most likely manage only two items at best, but some older children can master a three-item juggling act.

- Play with simple toys that require imagination only. No batteries or electrical outlets or screens allowed! Make up relays or challenges with bean bags or a lightweight, eight- to nine-inch-diameter ball. Or write a play with stuffed animals or dolls as the main characters.

- Fly a kite on a windy day but write love notes with markers on the kite and kite tail before sending it into the air. Tell your child, "Your love makes my heart soar!" and "Your love lifts me higher" and "I love you to the sky and back!"

- Play with old-fashioned toys. Learn a few yo-yo tricks or play a game of pick-up sticks or jacks.

- Play with a spray bottle of water outside. Let your child water the plants, draw on the sidewalk with chalk and wash it away, or paint a picture with watercolors on a large sheet of white paper pinned to an easel (spread old newspapers under the easel to catch drips) and then spray with water to watch the paint run and create a new masterpiece of paint drippings.

- Fill a wading pool with water and various water-safe toys and let your child explore floating and nonfloating. As always, never leave your child unattended near water. While playing in the water with your child, say, "I love spending time with you!"

- Read a favorite children's book backward, starting from the last page and ending at the first. Then share backward affirmations—for example, "Happy so me make you" or "Player baseball great a are you." Let each person share three or four to each family member.

- Switch out the toys in the sandbox frequently but surprise your child with the contents each time. If you don't have a sandbox, keep a bag near the door with outdoor-safe items and toys. Switch them out randomly to surprise your child when heading outside for playtime. Use a variety of measuring spoons and cups one day, then switch to funnels, strainers, and sieves the next day. Add plastic bowls and cups on occasion and construction vehicles another day. Oh, and be sure to write a new love note each time to place inside the sandbox or bag.

- Use low-tack painter's tape to create a highway or neighborhood on the floor. Play with toy cars and vehicles on the roads. Use additional tape to make a racetrack and race small cars across the floor!

- Read Bible stories with your child. Remind your child often how much God loves them.

EIGHT

. . . when we're serving others

- Have a time of dress-up with your child. When it's time to reorganize your closet and pass along clothes to another owner, let your child wear your or your spouse's clothes and pretend to be one of you or parade around the room or act out a silly play. After dress-up time, wash any clothes that need cleaning, press those that might have gotten wrinkled during playtime, fold neatly, and have your child accompany you to a secondhand store to donate the gently used clothing.

- Help your child write a thank-you note to the author of their favorite book. Encourage your child to share their favorite part with the author and tell why the book is treasured. Thank the author for writing books for children. Find the author's email address on a website or connect through the author's website contact page. Point out to your child that while you hope they'll get a personal response, not everyone has the chance to respond to letters. You'll have fun knowing that you personally thanked a favorite author!

- Volunteer together to ring a charity bell during the Christmas holidays. Be sure to take coins with you to drop in the collection receptacle. Keep extra coins in your purse or pocket throughout the season and let your child deposit coins each time you pass someone ringing a bell. Give your child a big hug and say, "I love to see you serving others!"

- Wear rubber gloves and clean up litter along the side of the road in your neighborhood or in a nearby park. Always be cognizant of moving vehicles—try to pick a time of day with very little traffic on the road. Tell your child, "I love you so much that I want the world around you to be litter-free and beautiful!"

- Make care kits for the homeless and keep the kits in the car to hand out to those in need. Say to your child, "I'm glad you're part of my family, and I want us to help someone who might not have a family member to take care of them right now." Make sure the items you purchase are individually wrapped and choose travel sizes of toiletries, when available. Let your child help you shop for the following items to place in gallon-sized resealable bags: small water bottle, hard candy or gum, lip balm, hand lotion, hand wipes, crackers, fruit snacks, protein bars, toothbrush, toothpaste, deodorant, and a pair of socks. Be sure to include a handwritten note or a hand-drawn picture.

- Make a habit of returning abandoned shopping carts to the nearest storage rack with your child's help. As the cart is rolling along, say, "I wheel love you forever!"

- Volunteer to walk dogs, play with puppies, or pet kittens at an animal shelter. When you leave the shelter, say to your child, "I think you're purrrrfect for our family!" or "Life without you would be ruff!"

- Teach your child to hold the door open for others when running errands or grocery shopping. After holding the door for another person, make eye contact with your child, give a wink with each eye, and say, "You know something? I a-door you!"

- Feed the birds in the winter using one of many homemade birdfeeder suggestions found online. Try different birdfeeders in various locations in the yard to see which the birds like best. Spend Saturday mornings or Sunday afternoons sitting quietly on a blanket in the yard or on a porch swing watching for winged visitors.

- Allow someone to go ahead of you when standing at the end of the checkout line in the grocery store. Talk about the following verse with your child while waiting your turn: "Do everything in love" (1 Cor. 16:14).

- Rake an elderly neighbor's yard together or shovel the walkway after a snowstorm. Compliment your child often during the chore with these words: "You're really a hard worker!" and "I love that you enjoy helping others!"

- Teach your child to include others on the playground. While visiting a park, encourage your child to invite a child who's alone to accompany them on the swing set. Say, "I love when you include others in playtime!"

- Donate outgrown baby clothes to a women's shelter, but first sort through the clothes with your child and share memories of each outfit and your child's baby days. After reminiscing, let your child help carry the clothes to the car and accompany you to donate them.

- Purchase two of each seasonal-apparel need in your child's size when the calendar months change and share the duplicates with others. For example, buy two pairs of gloves for winter, two pairs of rain boots for springtime, two bathing suits and two pairs of sunglasses for summer, and two windbreakers for the fall. Together, deliver the extras to a women's or homeless shelter or check with your child's school counselor for needs. Say to your child, "I love taking care of you so much that I want us to help another boy or girl to have what they need too!"

- Dine in a restaurant with your child and ask their favorite part of the meal. Be intentional about complimenting the server in front of your child, sharing what they liked best.

- Purchase several pairs of white socks that can be worn by men or women and let your child fill the toes with rolls of hard candy or mints. Tie a ribbon around each pair and attach a handwritten note to the ribbon for the recipient. Say to your child, "I am toe-tally in love with you" on the drive to a homeless shelter to drop off the socks.

- Bake cookies together to deliver to local first responders. On the drive to deliver the cookies, talk about your child's health and safety and how important both are to you. Say, "I like keeping you healthy and safe, so I want us to treat those who help keep the community healthy and safe.

- Verbally reward an especially helpful salesclerk while shopping with your child. Ask to speak to that person's manager and share details of the person's assistance and your appreciation for the stellar customer service.

- Volunteer to babysit a newborn for a couple of hours with your child's help while the new mom has special time with an older sibling. Say to your child, "I loved you before you were born, I loved you when you were a baby, I love you now, and I'll love you forever! And God loves you even more than I do!"

- Weed the flower bed with your child and surprise their other parent with the treat! Nudge your child while working and whisper, "Weed make a great pair for always!"

- Donate gently worn or new clothing to an organization that helps foster kids. Include copies of your child's favorite book with each donation too.

- Double up on some items when shopping for school supplies together and donate them to a women's or homeless shelter, a fostering organization, a church that meets the needs of kids, or to your child's teacher.

- Call a local nursing home and ask if you can visit during a meal to talk with some of the residents. Eat before you go so that you can focus all your attention on those at the table with you. Encourage your child to chat with the residents also.

- Make and share treats for the holidays with your child and don't forget those who might get overlooked, such as school and church custodians, the bus driver, the mail carrier, the dance teacher's assistant, the lonely widow down the street, the librarian, or your favorite pharmacist.

- Donate copies of favorite picture books to your child's pediatrician. Let your child write a note in the front that says something like this, "I hope you enjoy this book as much as I do!"

- Read together the latest edition of your child's favorite magazine, then donate the magazine to a hospital for use in the waiting room or to a teacher with a note that suggests they share it with a child in the classroom who could use a special treat.

- Talk with a church receptionist to get the name of a college student or single parent who could use some extra attention. Invite the student or family over for a meal.

- Purchase new packages of crayons and several coloring books. Help your child color one page in each book and write "I hope you feel better soon" on the page. Deliver the crayons and coloring books to a children's hospital.

- Write notes and cards to deployed servicemen and servicewomen. Be sure to thank them for their service and for providing protection for the country. Find addresses online from a reputable website and mail the cards accordingly.

- Volunteer to serve together at a soup kitchen. Wink at your child often and, when you're driving

home, say, "I think you're souper-fantastic!" and
"You were a souper helper today!"

• Make a charitable contribution in your child's
name to instill ownership in a cause. Have
your child pull money out of their piggy bank
and add some of your money to it. Explain in
detail what the donation will be used for and
periodically update your child on the work of the
organization.

NINE

. . . *when we're celebrating the seasons*

- Bake and decorate a gingerbread house together. Spray the house with varnish to preserve it, following the directions on the bottle. Then place the house on a countertop you don't use often with plans to leave it on display all year. One day each month, add decorations and embellishments to the scene to match the season.

- Take your child shopping for the other parent, a sibling, a grandparent, or a friend for gifts related to silly holidays you can find online. For example, look for a new hat or stocking cap for National Hat Day, purchase pizza together for National Cheese Pizza Day, or buy some colored erasers to acknowledge National Eraser Day.

- Go berry picking, fruit picking, nut picking, and vegetable picking according to the season. Work together in the kitchen with a new recipe to make use of each season's harvest. As *corny* as it sounds, make sure to say, "I love you berry much!" or "You're the apple of my eye!" or "I'm nuts about you!" or "No one can squash my love for you!"

- Be on the lookout for the first sign of fall colors in the treetops. Pick out a hardwood tree close to home and observe the changes each day when passing by. Take a leisurely drive over the weekend to look for more fall colors. Say to your child, "I've fallen for you!" or "I fall more in love with you every day!"

- Go for a walk on a crisp fall afternoon to collect colorful leaves. Carry along a resealable bag for the treasures. Select freshly fallen leaves or pluck one or two carefully from vibrant trees. Soon after returning from the walk, preserve the pretty leaves using one of several methods. View ways online or try this very simple one: Lay a sheet of paper towel on an ironing board and cover it with a piece of wax paper. Then spread the leaves in a single layer on top. Cover the leaves with another piece of wax paper, then another sheet of paper towel. Press with a warm iron, making sure the iron does not touch the wax paper. Allow the sealed paper time to cool, then cut the individual leaves apart. You can also press the leaves between two sheets of thick white paper with heavy books stacked on top. Keep the leaves covered for at least a week. For a more vibrant preserving of color, use a craft-store decoupage solution and paint each side of a fresh leaf with time for drying between sides.

• Go for a hayride with neighborhood families.

• Attend a community or church fall festival and play every game available.

• Visit a sunflower farm, navigate a corn maze, or explore a pumpkin patch. Be sure to take home several pumpkins to decorate. Spend an evening painting pumpkins and embellishing them with hair bows, paper-made sunglasses, ribbons, or yarn.

• Host a bonfire and make s'mores. As always, use precaution with little ones around an open fire and never leave kids unattended around a fire. Be sure to whisper in your child's ear, "I plan to love you s'more and s'more."

• Make caramel-apple treats. Cut an apple into slices that are one-half-inch thick. Insert a wooden popsicle stick into the bottom of each slice so that it resembles an "apple slice lollipop." Lay the handled slices on top of wax paper. Drizzle melted chocolate and melted caramel on each slice and sprinkle crushed nuts or chopped candy pieces on the drizzles while still warm and melted. Allow time to harden, then carefully lift from the paper and nibble away!

• Let your child pick out flower bulbs from a garden store in the fall. Plant the bulbs following the instructions on the package, then anticipate their arrival in springtime!

• Be prepared for the first cold day of winter that requires a coat with a prewritten love note, such as "You warm my heart!" or "You are one cool kid!" or "I love your warm hugs!" Stuff the note in a pocket before sending your child off to school or daycare or outside to play.

• Spend some creative time with your child on New Year's Day. Label twenty-four envelopes with the months of the year, two envelopes for each month. Spread craft paper and art supplies on a worktable. Have your child create a dozen notes or art projects, according to their age and abilities, and show them how to fold and stuff them into twelve of the envelopes. In the meantime, write your child a dozen love notes that include artwork and stuff your letters into the other twelve envelopes. Store the envelopes in a place where you'll see them as a reminder to open the appropriate envelopes on the first day of each new month.

• Go sledding in the winter. Use manufactured sleds but also try out unique ones, such as baking sheets, plastic trash-can lids, and large pieces of cardboard.

• Take your child on a sleigh ride. If that's not an option, load a wagon with blankets and let your child snuggle into them. Pull your child along the sidewalk or a path and enjoy the beauty of winter.

• Learn to ice skate and roller skate and hold hands while doing so.

• Work together to build a "snowchild" and dress the creation in your child's clothes.

• Take part in a snowball fight. When exhaustion sets in, lie down in the snow and make snow angels. Use spray bottles that contain a mixture of water and a few drops of food coloring to embellish the snow angels to resemble you and your child and to create an abstract snow painting.

• Visit a botanical garden with your child in springtime and look for every color of the rainbow while there.

• Pick out spring flowers together from a garden center and plant them in the shape of a heart in the flower bed. Be sure to watch for the bulbs you planted in the fall to burst forth in color!

• Grab umbrellas for both of you and dance in the grass during a springtime rain shower!

• Dye and decorate eggs together and have an egg hunt.

• Start together and update regularly a nature journal for springtime sightings of butterflies, other insects, migrating birds, ripening berries, smiling flower faces and blooms, spring peeper frogs, and more. Store pictures on a cell phone or use paper and crayons to describe and illustrate the sightings.

- Climb trees together or hold your child's hand while walking across a fallen log.

- Roll down a hill on soft, fresh springtime grass. (As grass may stain clothing, both of you should dress in well-worn play clothes!)

- Wear mud shoes, hold hands, and wade in the shallow edges of a stream. Look for round, flat rocks and practice skipping rocks downstream. Say to your child, "You make life more fun!"

- Create a backyard, rainy-day symphony. Let your child help you gather and place pots, pans, and bowls turned upside down on the grass and dance to the rhythm of plip-plopping raindrops.

- Plan a day at the seashore or lake and build a sandcastle or some type of fun nature construction with your child. Tell them, "I shore do love you!"

- Plant a garden together that includes vegetables your child loves and a few they have never tried.

- Visit a water park, amusement park, or county fair in the summertime.

TEN

. . . when we're showing affection

- Say "I love you" lots and lots!

- Hug often and give kisses freely.

- Make physical contact with your child often during the day, such as a pat on the back when you walk past, a quick hug, a kiss on top of the head, a hand squeeze, a tickle, a gentle pinch on the cheek accompanied by a smooching sound, a loving shoulder squeeze, or any other love touch you can think of.

- Tickle your child's bare back with a feather.

- Sit on the couch with a pillow in your lap. Let your child stretch out on the couch with their head on the pillow to watch a favorite television show.

- Count kisses with your kiddo. Start with one kiss for your sweetie in the morning. Steal two kisses after breakfast and later grab three kisses. Keep kissing sporadically during the day until you make it to fifteen or twenty kisses before bedtime.

- Brush your child's hair. Say to them, "You are a beautiful child of God! He loves you, and so do I!" Share this verse with your child: "See how very much our Father loves us, for he calls us his children, and that is what we are!" (1 John 3:1 NLT).

- Let your child pick a favorite show and scratch or rub their back while you watch it together. Tell your child, "I love spending time with you!"

- Make every effort to speak to your child at eye level. Lean over to make eye contact or get down on your knees or squat on the floor or pull your child onto your lap while sitting in a rocking chair for eye-to-eye conversation. Sit in a chair and let your child stand in front of you, lift your child to a nearby countertop and stand in front of them, or let your child stand in a chair in front of you and hold on to them during the conversation.

- Decide together on a secret hand signal or motion that means "I love you." It could be something as simple as touching your thumb quickly to your pinkie to resemble a quick kiss or folding one hand in the other to signify a mini-hug. Use the signal with your child at various times of the day at home or in other locations.

- Hold your child in your lap or snuggle close on the couch. Touch each of their fingers and name something you love about them as you touch each one, giving five or ten reasons. Have them wriggle off both socks and as you wiggle each toe, spout off ten more reasons why you love your child.

- Get creative with kisses. Give kisses on each cheek, kisses on top of the head, butterfly kisses on a cheek or hand, nose-to-nose kisses, belly-button kisses, kisses on the neck while humming a familiar tune, raspberry kisses on the bottom of the feet, and all-over-the-face kisses that include the nose, chin, ears, eyebrows, eyelids, cheeks, and forehead.

- Rub lotion on your child's hands and feet just before bedtime or arms and legs after bath time.

- Give your child a manicure and pedicure and add polish, if desired.

- Ask to brush your child's teeth, even if they are old enough to do it themselves. While brushing say, "I love your smile" or "You make me smile, just by being you."

- Keep a small picture of your child on your keychain, place one prominently on your desk at home and work, keep one in your wallet, save lots of pictures of your child on your computer screensaver, place photos on the refrigerator, keep a snapshot in a car pocket, and place one on a bedside table. Frequently call attention to a photo and say, "I just love this picture of you! It reminds me of . . ." and share a fond memory about the picture. Then give your child a bear hug and kiss on the head. Say, "A picture is worth a thousand words, and I love you many more words than that!"

- Laugh at your child's jokes and riddles always, no matter how silly or ridiculous. Belly laugh with your child, then give them a big hug and squeeze, and say, "You are so much fun!" and "I love laughing with you!" and "I love the sound of your laughter!"

- Wink, smile, nod, and give your child a thumbs-up often, especially in public when they are across the room from you or on the soccer field or performing on stage.

- Give yourself a bear hug and point to them when your child is looking in your direction, which is a secret code for sending them a hug.

- Blow kisses to your child when you find yourself in the same location but not side by side. And be sure to "catch" all kisses that your child blows in return. In fact, if the opportunity presents itself, pretend the "kiss" is eluding you and chase, reach, jump, and snatch it out of the air. That's a surefire way to bring a smile to your child's face.

- Shampoo and blow dry your child's hair, even if your child is old enough to accomplish the task. Have them lie down on the kitchen counter next to the sink and give a fun shampoo and head massage. Brush, blow dry, and style their hair and say to your child, "I love every hair on your head! And if I love you that much, then just think how much God loves you! Because you know what it says in the Bible? 'And the very hairs on your head are all numbered'" (Luke 12:7 NLT).

- Give your child a foot massage, hand massage, scalp massage, shoulder massage, or back massage.

- Have your child lie on their stomach in bed at bedtime. Slide your child's pajama top up and "write" a message with your finger, one letter at a time, on their back. Let your child guess each letter. Spell out "I love you" or "Good night" or draw smiley faces for nonreaders.

- Sit cross-legged on the floor with your child, knees touching. Make up clapping and hand-touching rhythms.

- Wake your child in the morning or after a nap with a tickle-fest.

- Peel the sheets off your child's bed on laundry day, stretch out the flat sheet on top of the bed, and have your child lie near one edge. Let your child hang on to the edge of the sheet and roll them over and over in the sheet with only their head uncovered. Carry your "mummy-wrapped" child to the laundry room and help them wriggle out of the sheet.

- Hold your child's hand at times other than crossing the street or in a busy store. Hold their hand for no reason other than you want to. Swing your arms back and forth and say, "I really like spending time with you."

- Sit with bare feet close to the fireplace (or heat vent) during the wintertime. Drape your child's legs over yours so that all twenty toes are touching and watch the fire burn or talk about your favorite parts of the day.

- Wear a pair of fuzzy socks on your hands and rub your child's back, arms, and legs before bedtime.

- Let your child climb in bed with you to watch television. Swaddle the two of you in one blanket or sheet and lean against a pile of pillows to watch the show.

- Kiss and hug your spouse in front of your child. In your child's presence, hold hands with your spouse while running errands and put your arm around them in church.

ELEVEN

. . . when we're
sharing love notes

- Write affirmations on paper napkins while watching a movie one night after your child goes to bed. Here are a few suggestions: "I love you, you are precious to me," "I like how kind you are," "You're a great student," and "You are a blessing to this family." Then place them in the napkin holder to be used at mealtimes.

- Create an acrostic by writing your child's name vertically on a piece of paper. Use each letter to spell out things you love about your child. Tell your child how you picked out their name.

- Use dry-erase markers or lipstick to write a love note on your child's bathroom mirror when they are asleep or away.

- Thank your spouse frequently in your child's presence and be specific with your praise. Boast about your spouse.

- Learn "I love you" in seven different languages. Consistently use one language every Monday, a different one every Tuesday, and so on for the entire week. Make a habit of speaking the words daily to your child in the appropriate language.

- Write this note: "I love you from your head to your toes, and so does God." Fold the note and tuck it into your child's shoe.

- Compliment your child often. Affirm good choices, good grades, successful chore completion, kindness to a sibling or friend, and any other activity or character trait worth celebrating. Use specific examples, not generic ones, when complimenting—for example, "I really like that you shared your favorite stuffed animal with your little brother."

- Brag about your child's unique qualities to others in front of your child.

- Say "thank you" often to your child throughout the day and encourage them to do the same for you and others.

- Ask your child, "How was your day?" and listen intently to the answer. Ask about the best part of the day and find out the lowest part of the day too. Congratulate, celebrate, and cheer for the high points and offer condolences or suggestions for the low points. Pray, praising God for the day's special parts and asking for wisdom and guidance for the difficult parts of the day.

- Keep a picture frame on the bedside table in your child's room. Print pictures of your child, you and your child, or a family picture and change out the picture in the frame every couple of weeks. Leave love notes next to the picture for your child to find first thing in the morning or at night before they go to sleep.

- Attach a note to a piggy bank or coin-collecting jar that says, "I'm saving all my love for you." Deposit change throughout the month into the container, and at the end of the month, empty it and count the coins. Then use the money for a treat, such as ice cream or a movie or a new picture book or a puzzle—something you'll enjoy doing together.

- Write a love letter to your child or pick out a sappy card and express your sentiments on the inside of the card. Then tuck the letter or card in an envelope along with a page of heart stickers, address it to your child, and draw hearts on the outside of the envelope. Drop the letter in the mail. When it arrives, make a big deal about going through the mail and announcing that your child has a letter.

- Share a love-note journal with your child. Write a note or letter in a bound journal (or draw a picture with an "I love you" message for a younger child) and place the journal on a pillow or bedside table. Write positive messages, notes of affirmation, congratulatory notes on a recent accomplishment, reasons why you love them, or things you pray for them, and be sure to include the date of the message. Encourage your child to respond in the next day or so with a note or letter (or simple picture for a younger child) and to return the journal to your bedside table or pillow. Once the journal is filled, pack it away for a keepsake and start a new one.

- Draw a heart or write "I love you" on a steamy bathroom mirror when your child is away from home. The next time they shower, the message will reappear on the foggy mirror.

- Draw a large heart and write "I love you" with chalk on the sidewalk or driveway while your child is at school or taking a nap.

- Tear off a strip of aluminum foil and crumple it into a heart shape. Hide the foil heart in your child's room where they will easily discover it, such as inside a sock drawer or under a pillow.

- Keep sticky notepads in a variety of colors on hand and write notes often. Stick the love messages on your child's bedroom door, the bathroom mirror, the back of their dining room chair, the inside lid of a lunch box, the inside cover of a schoolbook, the lid of a toy box, or any other random location you can think of.

- Give small trinkets and inexpensive gifts, accompanied by love notes, to go with silly daily celebrations. For example, give your child a package of sharpened pencils for National

Pencil Day with a note that says, "I love you—
get the point?" Or celebrate National Tape
Measure Day with the gift of a tape measure
and a note that says, "My love for you is
beyond measure!"

- Hide love notes in your child's backpack or
  suitcase whenever they travel away from
  home, whether to their grandparents' for an
  afternoon or an overnight stay or to a friend's
  for a sleepover. Hide several notes in different
  locations, expressing your love and admiration.
  Similarly, when you travel for business or
  pleasure and the little one stays behind, be
  sure to write at least one love note for every
  day you'll be gone and have your spouse or
  the child's caregiver share the notes on the
  appropriate days.

- Write on the first line of a sheet of paper "Thank
  you for . . ." and use a magnet to hold it on the
  refrigerator. Add messages periodically for no
  reason or for special occasions, such as for
  "being kind to others" or "cleaning up your room
  today without being told."

- Post a lawn sign when your child is away from home visiting a relative for the day, playing with friends, or attending school. Use an old garage sale sign with metal prongs for sticking into the lawn. Cover the original sign with poster board or a strip of freezer paper or brown wrapping paper. Write "Welcome home, I love you!" on the sign and display it in a prominent location for your child's return home.

- Encourage your child's map-reading skills and share a love note simultaneously. Draw a simple map of the neighborhood and place a heart sticker where your house is located. Write this message below the heart, "Home is where the love is."

- Carve a heart shape into your child's bar of bath soap.

- Stamp out a large heart shape in the snow after your child has gone to bed (but make sure no additional snowfall is predicted during the night).

- Trace around a pair of your child's shoes to make shoeprint patterns. Then use construction paper or other colored paper to cut out enough prints to make a long trail in the house. After your child falls asleep, place the shoeprints in a trail from your child's bedroom door to another location in the house. Leave love notes along the path, and at the end of the prints, leave a small gift, such as a new puzzle or coloring book or another treat. Or leave a note that says, "Get dressed! We're going to the park!" or "Meet me in the den, and let's play a board game!"

- Save newspapers for an extended period. Once you've accumulated a large stack, pick an evening to compose love notes to each other. Cut headlines into individual words and use the words to compose short love messages or sentences of affirmation to each other.

- Smear a thin layer of shaving cream on the bathroom mirror and write "I love you" with your finger in the cream.

- Use shoe polish or car window paint to write a love note or draw a heart on the car window nearest your child's seat. Do this when your child is asleep or away from home and surprise them on the next car ride.

- Purchase a dozen inexpensive flowers with long stems. Place a vase on the kitchen table with water inside and a note next to the vase that says, "You fill my heart with love!" Tape a love note onto the stem of each flower, near the top and close to the bloom, that begins, "I love you because . . ." Finish the sentence with something specific about your child. Then distribute the flowers in twelve locations where your child will easily find them—for example, on their pillow, the bathroom sink, and their desk. Encourage your child to place the flowers in the vase with each finding.

- Purchase a box of fortune cookies from the grocery store. With tweezers, carefully remove the slip of paper inside of the cookies. (You may need to gently shake the cookie to allow the enclosed strip of paper to slip through the opening.) Replace them with personalized love notes for your child. Return the cookies to the package and glue the box closed to give the appearance of an unopened package of fortune cookies.

TWELVE

. . . *when we're vacationing*

- Be tourists for a day in your hometown, no matter how long you've lived there. Take your child sightseeing and snap lots of pictures. Use some feature of each location to express affection to your child. For example, when you pass a farm or stable, say, "I love you like a horse loves hay." When you spot a railroad crossing sign, say, "I love you like a train loves tracks." A post office? "I love you like a letter loves a stamp." Hopefully, your child will catch on and make up their own love messages back to you!

- Go tent camping. Plan a variety of excursions and take in the sights and related activities of the location. Camp indoors, in the backyard, in a grandparents' backyard, at a nearby park, at a campsite on the beach, in the mountains, at an amusement park, or any other creative location that comes to mind. For some spots, you'll need to check that camping is permitted. Keep a camping journal and update it after each trip.

- Take a mystery day trip or vacation. Choose an adventure you know your child will enjoy, such as a trip to the beach or to a museum or on a hike in the forest. Pack any necessary items your child will need for the adventure. Don't reveal the surprise until you arrive at the destination.

• Never pass up a photo-booth opportunity. Step inside the booth with your child to make fun, silly memories. Look for photo booths at fairs, amusement parks, weddings, tourist locations, and other spots. Save and date the snapshots and use magnets to place them on the refrigerator.

• Prepare for a long trip by taking along several individually wrapped special gifts, such as a new book, a coloring book and crayons, a package of stickers and blank paper, or other activity options. Write love notes on the outside of each gift. Hand your child a new treat at designated mile markers or geographic locations.

• Print a map of the United States. Keep the map and some crayons in the car. While traveling, look at license plates, and when you spot a new tag, invite your child to color the corresponding state. Then make up a silly love quote alliteration about that state—for example, "I love you more than the mountains in Montana" and "I wish you waves of wonder in Washington."

• Drop pebbles over the side of a bridge into a river
  or creek and listen for the kerplop! Or drop small
  sticks on the upstream side of a bridge, and then
  run to the other side to watch them float past.
  Try to spot darting fish or diving turtles. Say, "My
  love for you is deeper than the deepest river" or
  "There's nothing fishy about my love for you" or
  "I shell love you forever!"

• Visit a petting zoo with your child.

• Travel to a large zoo that you know has an exhibit
  of your child's favorite wild animal. Look for
  animals from A to Z and try to learn something
  new about several of them. If a trip to the zoo
  is out of the question, take a virtual tour with
  educational websites. Say to your child, "You have
  a zest for learning!"

• Visit an aquarium and be sure to stop at a tank
  that allows your child to pet a stingray. If you
  don't live near an aquarium, consider setting up
  a small one in your home and let your child name
  all the fish in the tank. Or visit a pet store with a
  large aquarium on display.

- Explore a nearby children's museum. Plan to spend as much time as possible there and actively join your child in their exploits. Snap lots of pictures to save as reminders of the day's fun.

- Ask a farmer for permission to search for animal tracks on their land. Before traveling to the farm, study animal tracks online or check out a book from the library with identifiers of animal tracks. Walk and explore the fields, sandy areas, and pond edges and watch for signs of wildlife. Look for tracks of deer, raccoons, wild turkeys, coyotes, slithering snakes, turtles, and other forest or field animals.

- Go on an architectural adventure downtown. Before the adventure, stop by the library with your child to become familiar with architectural vocabulary. Learn what a balconet, canopy, casement, cupola, dormer, parapet, transom, and turret are. Learn about the three major column styles: Corinthian, Ionic, and Doric. Then go for a walk downtown and see how many designs you and your child can spot on government buildings, theaters, storefronts, and old homes.

- Make a list of things you might see and attach words or actions to those sightings before a long car ride. For example, if you see a bird, you flap your arms like wings. An eighteen-wheeler sighting is a prompt to say, "I'll love you a long time!" A deer in the distance invites you to say, "You are my favorite dear!" Come up with age-appropriate things to remember and do for your child and have fun on the journey. Just remember that the driver needs to keep their hands on the steering wheel, and activities need to be seatbelt and car-seat approved!

- Let your child name the family car or the train or bus or subway taken most often.

- Keep a sunset journal together. Snap a picture and journal about what you see. Take a selfie in

the backyard at sunset, print out the picture to tape in the journal, date the page, and tell about the event. Watch the sunset from a variety of locations downtown, around the city, and in the countryside. Drive to nearby towns and do the same. Watch the sunset from the top of a mountain, at a lake, or near the ocean. Watch a sunset from a rooftop or from an amusement park. Keep the journal as a family album.

- Play miniature golf, bowl a round or two, ski down a mountain, race in go-carts, pedal a paddleboat, go snow tubing, ride a roller coaster, and find other high-adventure activities to add childhood memories.

- Never miss a parade! Take your child to local ones and not-so-local ones and watch televised ones together. Then decorate a kiddie wagon like a float for an at-home parade! You can even ask other kids and parents in the neighborhood to join you with their own wagon or bike floats!

- Go to a horse show or circus event, then gallop with your child to and fro in the front yard when you get home. And be sure to go horseback riding—whether it's on the back of a living, breathing horse or around and around on a carousel. Say to your child, "You make my heart gallop!"

• Attend an outdoor concert, high school band concert, or symphony performance. Do you play a musical instrument? Teach your child a few notes or a simple song. Give your child a wink and say, "Take note of this—I will love you forever!" After a chuckle from your child about the silly pun, add, "But seriously—aren't we glad that God's love never ends? Let's memorize Psalm 136:26 together. It says, 'Give thanks to the God of heaven. His love endures forever.'"

• Enjoy a professional ballet performance, local dance recital, or other cultural event with your child. Take snacks if allowed and bring with you a picture book or sticker page to entertain little ones while waiting. Keep the experiences positive and age-appropriate to encourage a lifelong love of such events.

• Go fishing. Take a selfie with your catch and release it back into the water for another day.

- Pack pillows, blankets, and snacks and go to a movie with your child at an old-fashioned drive-in theater.

- Search for four-leaf clovers in a pasture, heart-shaped leaves in the forest, or sand dollars at the beach. When you find one, bow or curtsy to your child and say, "For you, my lady" or "For you, sir."

- Tour a cave with your child to see stalactites and stalagmites and other cool underground sights.

- Visit a pond or creek and give your child a small net to catch a minnow, tadpole, or crayfish. Put the tiny critter in a jar with water and watch it swim for a few minutes. Then release the animal back into the pond or creek to swim away.

- Pull out photos from the previous year's trip before leaving for vacation. Talk to your child about that adventure and share favorite memories and funny happenings.

- Visit a butterfly garden or bird sanctuary. Which butterfly or bird was your favorite? Your child's favorite?

- Take in as many water activities as your location or summer vacation allows: wade in a stream, swim in the ocean, take pictures of a waterfall, dip toes in a lake, go fishing in a pond, paddle a kayak, play in a backyard kiddie pool, and swim in a public pool.

- Make a bucket list of sights to see before your child is a tweenager. That list may include specific locations but also consider such sights as a windmill, lighthouse, working farm, fruit orchard, dude ranch, silo, tunnel, skyscraper, historical markers, and more. When going on a vacation or trip, plan detours along the way to mark one or more items off your bucket list.

a letter to parents

Dearest guardian of God's treasured children,

Let's face it—parenting can be the toughest job on the planet, but it is certainly the most rewarding one! And time spent with our little ones is fleeting . . . What's that saying? "The days are long, but the years are short."

Be sure to make the most of every opportunity to make memories with your kids. You won't regret later that you sometimes went to bed with a sinkful of dirty dishes, but you may wish you'd spent more time outside playing with your children or reading that book "just one more time."

The moments don't have to be monumental to be momentous! You know what my kids remember most about a couple of our vacations? Jumping from one bed to the other bed in the hotel room! And not only did Mommy and Daddy encourage and take part in the fun, but we also piled pillows on the floor and stood between the beds to make sure no one got hurt.

Little moments add up to big memories! Encourage them, create them, be part of them every day.

Big moments in a family are fun too and should be celebrated with great fanfare!

In other words, nothing is too big or too small when it comes to expressing love to our children. Love your children with great gusto. You'll make memories to last a lifetime, and you'll give them a glimpse of how big the love of their heavenly Father is!

And on those days when you think you've barely had time to breathe, let alone make "lasting memories," then give yourself grace and realize that you'll have another opportunity the next day. Parenting is hard—you're doing a great job! Keep up the good work.

With love and blessings and
prayers for memory making,
Julie

P.S. I'd love to hear some of your unique ways to say "I love you" to your child. Connect with me on social media and share your ideas!

Julie Lavender is the award-winning author of several books, including *365 Days of Celebration and Praise* and *Creative Sleepovers for Kids!*, and coauthor of *Come and Behold Him*. Her work has appeared in several anthologies and curricula, as well as many magazines, such as *The Upper Room, Guideposts, Homeschooling Today, ParentLife, Clubhouse, Today's Christian Woman*, and *Focus on the Family*. Julie has a master's degree in early childhood education, taught public school in three states, and delighted in homeschooling her four children in six states during her husband's navy career. She writes faith-based articles for her local newspaper and is a regular contributor to several websites and blogs on parenting topics. Julie lives with her husband, David, in South Georgia, not far from the charming city of Savannah.

GET TO KNOW
Julie

To connect with Julie and read her blog, head to

julielavenderwrites.com

Or follow her on social media!

  JulieLavenderAuthor

JLavenderwrites

julielavenderwrites